# KIDS SPRING CRAFTS

EMILY KINGTON

## SAFETY FIRST

- Some plants may sting or prick you, so ask an adult before touching.
- When using scissors and glue, you may need help from an adult.

## CARING FOR THE ENVIRONMENT

- Never go exploring on a scavenger or nature hunt without an adult.
- Try not to disturb or damage nature during a hunt.
- Try to avoid picking nature finds from trees and plants, mainly use things found on the ground.

When making the crafts in this book, use a tablecloth, cardboard, or newspaper to protect surfaces.

Look for this sign accompanying some of the craft instructions. You may need help from an adult with these tasks.

 EASY

 MEDIUM

HARDER

These icons are a guide to the difficulty level of each craft. They show you when you may need another pair of hands.

# CONTENTS

4  Spring Crafts

6  Materials

8  Flower Press Fun

10  Sowing Seeds in Spring

12  Happy Animal Magnets

14  Spring Chickens

18  Buzzy Beehive

22  Flowerpot Scarecrow

26  Lucky Clucking Puppets

28  Rainy Day Printing

# SPRING CRAFTS

New leaves on the trees, baby animals, and flowers in blossom are just a few of the things that make spring such an inspirational season for making some spectacular crafts.

The great thing about using nature finds and recycled materials is that they can be used in more than one project throughout the year, and it is all for free.

# WE ARE GOING ON A SCAVENGER HUNT!

It is spring, so it is time to pick flowers from your garden, discover spring animals, and collect other nature finds along the way. Create amazing decorations and crafts for spring. Remember to take a bag to carry all your finds home in.

## ABOUT SEASONAL CRAFTS

The following pages are packed with inspiring ideas for crafts to make in spring. You can follow them exactly, or make them your own by using different nature finds.

# MATERIALS

Spring is a great season for a nature scavenger hunt. Keep your eyes peeled for some interesting finds around where you live. Here is everything that was used to make all of the crafts in this book.

### HOUSEHOLD AND RECYCLED MATERIALS:

- Cereal box (or similar)
- Corrugated cardboard
- Flour
- Garden twine
- Kitchen sponge
- Large recycled lid (or baking tray)
- Polystyrene packaging
- Resealable food bags
- Strong cardboard box (such as a shoebox)
- Thick cardboard tube
- White stuffing (from an old pillow or toy)

### TOOLS AND CRAFT MATERIALS:

- Assorted paper
- Beads
- Cardboard
- Card
- Craft pegs
- Craft sticks
- Felt
- Flour
- Foam craft sheets
- Glue brush
- Magnets
- Mixing bowl
- Mixing spoon
- Paintbrush
- Paints
- Pair of scissors
- Pens/pencil
- Pipe cleaners
- Plastic eyes
- Pom poms
- Ruler
- School glue (PVA)
- String
- Strong glue
- Tissue paper
- Tracing paper
- Wooden skewer

Here are some ideas for nature finds:

Moss

Spring flowers and plants

Sticks/twigs

Soil

Flower seeds

Leaves

# FLOWER PRESS FUN

Use some books to make this simple flower press. It is fun and easy for anyone to do.

**YOU WILL NEED:**

- Resealable food bag
- Paper
- Tissue paper (optional)

**TOOLS:**
- School glue (PVA)
- Heavy books
- Pair of scissors

**1.** Spring is a great time to collect flowers to press, so it is the ideal time to go on a nature hunt.

**2.** Fold a sheet of paper in half (if you have tissue paper, first line the inside with it).

**TOP TIP:** Take a resealable bag to put them in to keep them fresh.

Tissue paper helps the flowers to dry, but remove it after two days and then continue to press the flowers directly between the folded paper.

**3.** Arrange your flowers and leaves on the paper, leaving plenty of space between them.

To press, put them inside the pages of a heavy book and then put more heavy books on top.

Add paper in between your book pages to avoid staining the book.

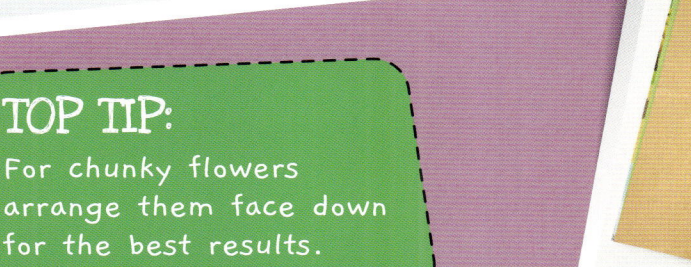

**TOP TIP:**
For chunky flowers arrange them face down for the best results.

**4.** You should press flowers and grasses for two weeks. Try not to peek at them before then.

**TOP TIP:**
If you gently paint your pressed flowers with school glue, it will keep them looking great for longer.

You can use pressed flowers in all kinds of crafts, so keep pressing all year round!

# SOWING SEEDS IN SPRING

Planting seeds in spring will give you plenty of flowers to press all summer long!

**YOU WILL NEED:**
- Soil
- Flour (any kind will do)
- Packets of seeds
- water

**TOOLS:**
- Large recycled lid or baking tray
- Mixing spoon
- Mixing bowl

1. Measure 10 parts of soil to 1 part of flour and mix them together.

2. Slowly add small amounts of water until the mixture comes together like a dough.

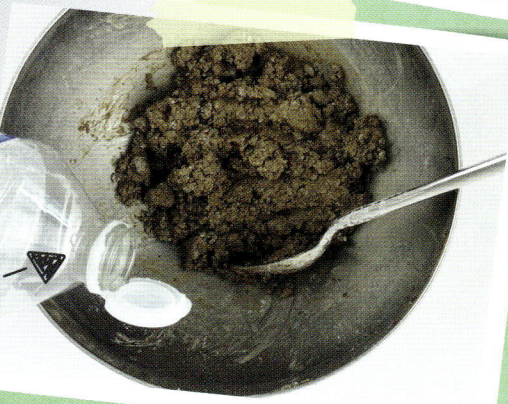

3. Using your hands, roll the soil mixture into small balls.

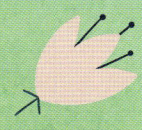

**4.** Open your seed packets and sprinkle the seeds onto the recycled lid or baking tray.

**5.** Roll the soil balls into the seeds and let dry for three days. Toss them into your garden and then wait for some beautiful summer suprises.

If you don't have a garden, you can plant seeds in flowerpots, which you can paint, too!

# HAPPY ANIMAL MAGNETS

Many animals are out and about in spring. These magnets are fun to make and useful, too!

### YOU WILL NEED:

- Recycled polystyrene
- Card
- String
- Pipe cleaners
- White stuffing (from an old pillow or toy)
- Mini pom poms
- Magnets
- Plastic eyes

### TOOLS:

- School glue (PVA)
- Marker pen
- Pair of scissors

**1.** 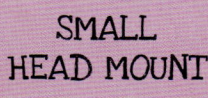 Trim polystyrene into a round body and make a small mount for the head.

SMALL HEAD MOUNT

Glue some magnets onto the back of the polystyrene body.

**2.** Seal the polystyrene mounts by painting them with school glue. This will stop the polystyrene from breaking up.

# SPRING CHICKENS

You can make a funky chicken nesting box. It will be perfect for celebrating spring.

**YOU WILL NEED:**
- Cardboard/card
- Craft paper (or paint for decorating box)
- Strong box (such as a shoebox)
- Craft sticks
- White stuffing (from an old pillow or toy)
- Plastic eyes
- Nature finds

**TOOLS:**
- Strong glue
- Pair of scissors
- Ruler (for measuring the box)

1. Draw a chicken design on paper with different parts: head, body, beak, and eyes.

Mount for the beak

Mount for the head

2. Copy the different chicken parts onto bright craft paper, then cut out the parts.

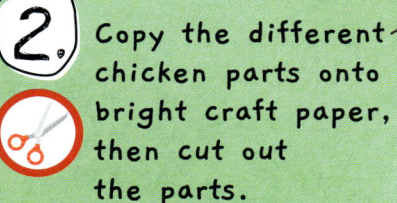

3. Make some cardboard mounts and glue the beak, eyes, and body to them. They will make the parts stand out.

**4.** Glue the chicken parts together as shown, and add fluffy stuffing.

**5.** To make a shelf, measure the inside of your box (width by depth). Draw a rectangle with the same measurements onto a piece of cardboard and cut it out.

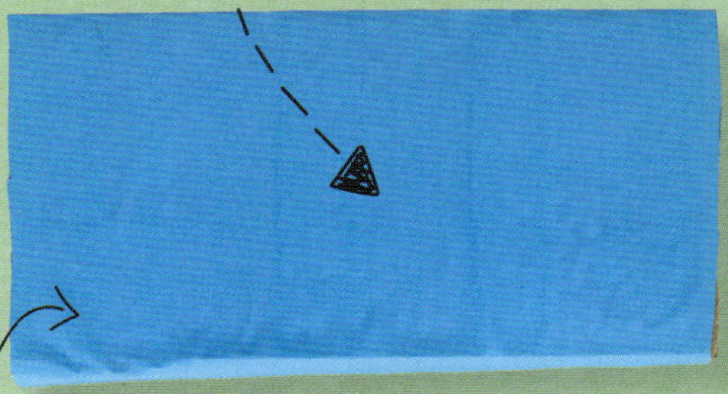

Cover your shelf with bright paper, or paint it.

**6.** Decorate the inside of the box with bright paper or paint.

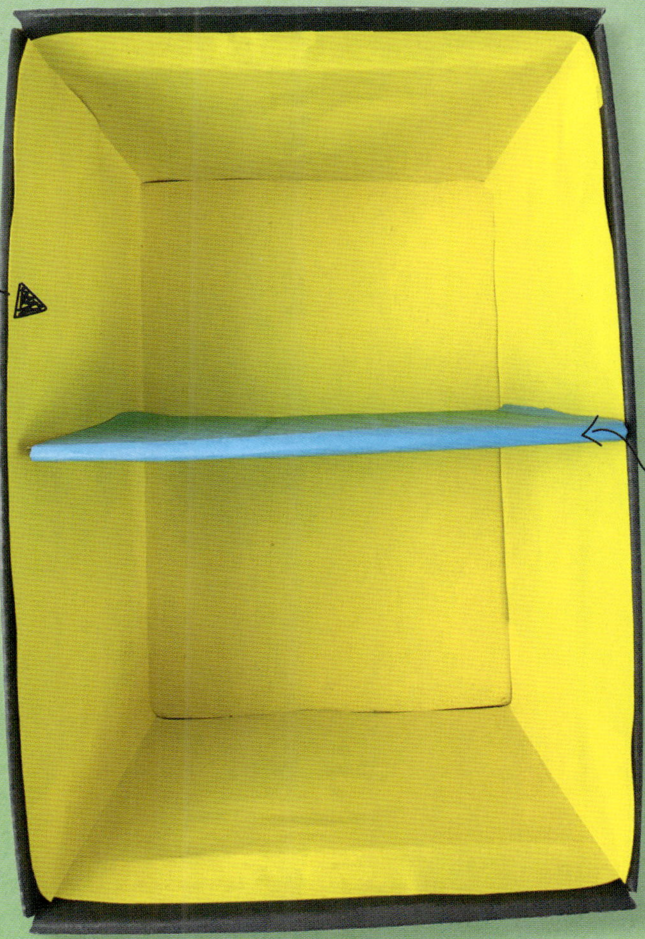

Using strong glue, fix the shelf into the middle of the box.

15

**7.** Make a fence with craft sticks for a chicken to nest behind.

Plan how many craft sticks you will need for your box. Your box may not be the same size.

✂ Cut craft sticks to 7.5-cm (3-inch) lengths. Glue them vertically to four horizontal craft sticks, as shown above.

**8.** Make three funky chickens to nest in your box and glue them into place before decorating the box.

This chicken has a cardboard mount glued to the wall to make it stand out.

Draw your own eyes or use plastic eyes.

16

# BUZZY BEEHIVE

Did you know a busy bumblebee can visit up to 6,000 flowers on a sunny day?

**YOU WILL NEED:**

- Yellow, black, and beige pipe cleaners
- Plastic eyes
- Tracing paper
- Cardboard box
- Felt
- String

**TOOLS:**
- Paintbrush/pens
- Pencil
- Paint
- Pair of scissors
- Strong glue

1. To make a bumblebee, make rings out of pipe cleaners. Wrap a pipe cleaner around a paintbrush or pen, twist it around itself, and trim off the end.

Use a smaller brush/pen to make two small rings for each end.

Tiny face molded from pipe cleaner.

Make five rings of alternating colours.

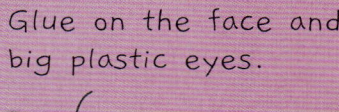

Glue on the face and big plastic eyes.

SMALL

LARGE

2. Slip the rings off and glue them all together at the twisted end.

3. Make the antennae by trimming the fluffy surface from a black pipe cleaner and mold it into shape, then glue them between the eyes.

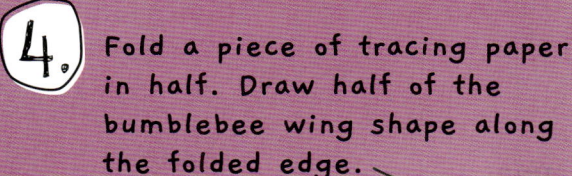

**4.** Fold a piece of tracing paper in half. Draw half of the bumblebee wing shape along the folded edge.

BUMBLEBEE WINGS

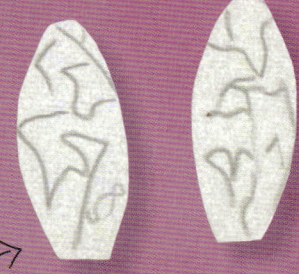

HONEYBEE WINGS

 Cut out and unfold the tracing paper wings. Then draw on veins with a pencil.

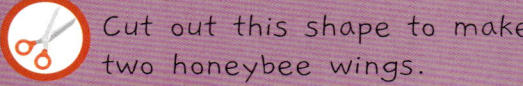 Cut out this shape to make two honeybee wings.

**5.** A honeybee has a thinner body than a bumblebee, so use smaller brushes/pens to make the rings for its body.

**6.** Glue the wings in among the rings.

HONEYBEE

Make three honeybees. Then glue each of your bees onto pipe cleaners like this.

19

Did you know, a honeybee produces about a teaspoon of honey in their lifetime and they have FIVE eyes!

Glue your bees around the hive.

You can decorate your hive with dried flowers from your flower press (see pages 8-9).

# FLOWERPOT SCARECROW

Scarecrows are supposed to scare birds away from crops. This one is too cute for that, but it is fun to have around.

**YOU WILL NEED:**

- Garden string
- Coloured String
- 1 stick
- Sponge
- Moss
- Bead (or similar)
- Plastic eyes
- Felt
- Pipe cleaner (mouth)
- Wooden skewer

**TOOLS:**
- Strong glue
- Pair of scissors

1. Fray some garden string, to glue to the end of the arms.

2. For the arms, find a stick that has a curve similar to this one.

3. Glue the frayed string to each end of the arms. Wrap string around the stick to make it look like a striped jumper.

**4.** Cut a circular shape from a large sponge about the size of a table tennis ball.

**5.** Wrap the string around the sponge as shown, crossing over the middle each time. Doing this will build the shape of a face. Cover the sponge completely.

**6.** Cut a triangle shape out of the sponge to make a hat that fits the head.

Tie some string around part of the sponge to make it look like a hat as shown.

**7.** Glue some moss on top of the head for the hair.

Glue the hat to the moss.

Add plastic eyes, a bead (or something similar) for the nose, and a small piece of pipe cleaner for the mouth.

8. Attach the back of the head to a long wooden skewer, using strong glue.

Then glue on the arms just below the head.

9. To make a coat for your scarecrow, cut out two felt rectangles the right length for your scarecrow's body.

Cut a hole in each piece, about a third of the way down.

10. Slip the arms of the scarecrow through the holes in the felt.

Wrap the felt around the scarecrow's middle and tie with string for the belt.

How cool does the scarecrow look? Inside or outside, your scarecrow will make you smile!

Stick your scarecrow into a flowerpot.

# LUCKY CLUCKING PUPPETS

It's the chick and chicken show! These homemade puppets are a lot of fun to make.

### YOU WILL NEED:
- Coloured felt
- Pipe cleaner
- Stuffing (from an old pillow or toy)

### TOOLS:
- Strong glue
- Pair of scissors

**1.** To make puppets that will fit your hand, fold a piece of felt in half and draw around your hand, as shown.

Then draw an arch shape bigger than your hand.

**2.** Glue around the sides and top of the felt to join the pieces together. Do not glue the bottom, because this is where your hand goes in.

Cut around the arch shape to make the front and back of your puppet (two pieces of arch-shaped felt).

# RAINY DAY PRINTING

Spring has sunny days, but also rainy days. This smart printing craft will keep the rainy day blues away!

## YOU WILL NEED:

- Thick cardboard tube (from cling film or similar)
- Coloured foam craft sheets
- Acrylic paints
- Craft paper
- Craft pegs
- Wooden skewer
- Pressed flowers (see page 8-9)

### TOOLS:
- Pair of scissors
- School glue (PVA)
- Paintbrush

**1.** Brush a coat of paint over a sheet of foam. This is white paint on red foam.

**2.** Starting in the top left corner, place the end of the tube on the painted foam. Drag it down and lift it off the surface to make a tubular pattern. Repeat until you reach the end of the sheet.

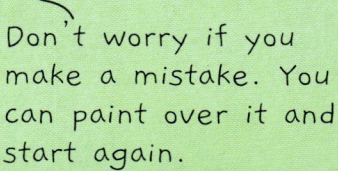

Don't worry if you make a mistake. You can paint over it and start again.

**3.** With clean hands, carefully lay the painted side of the foam down onto your craft paper. Press it down.

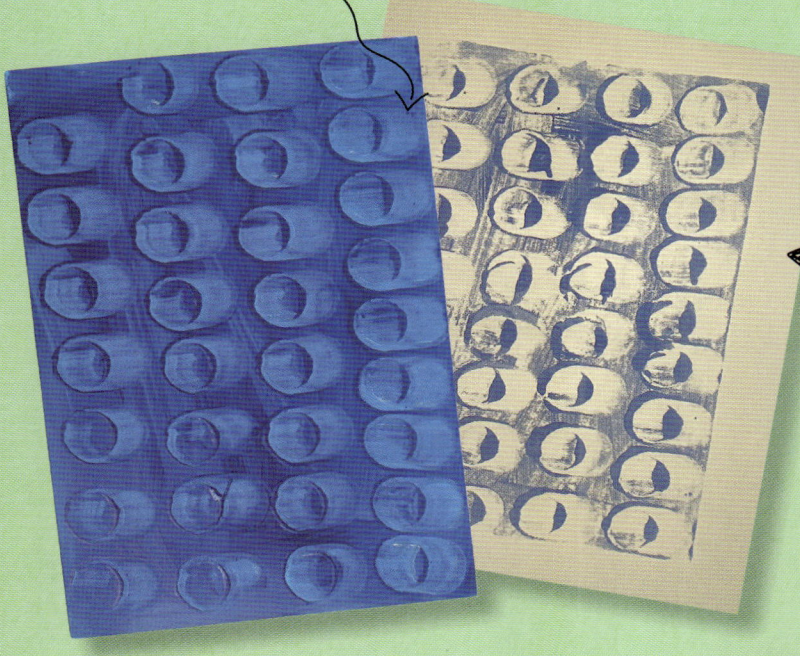

Carefully peel the foam back and let both the reverse print on paper and the foam sheet dry.

This is blue paint on a blue foam sheet.

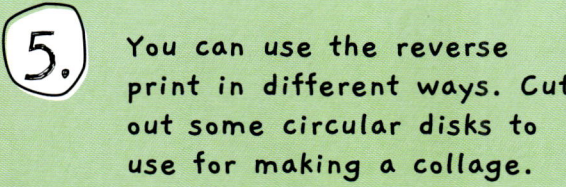

**4.** Do more reverse prints using different coloured foam sheets and paint. Keep both the reverse prints and the foam to use as backgrounds!

**5.** You can use the reverse print in different ways. Cut out some circular disks to use for making a collage.

**6.** You can also use dried flowers as a centrepiece for your collage.

**TOP TIP:**
Play around with the design before you glue everything down.

**7.** Glue your collage pieces down.

**TOP TIP:**
Use both your reverse printed papers and the foam sheets to see what different effects you can get!

**8.** Create different prints using both craft and nature things.

Add bubbles by dipping the flat end of a skewer or something similar into bright blue paint and dot it onto the foam.

Small craft pegs make great transfer prints of robotic fish against the tubular background.

The blue foam print is great for creating an underwater scene!

Use the same peg over and over again. Just re-paint the peg with different colours and press it onto the foam.

Copyright © 2023 Hungry Tomato Ltd

First published in 2023 by Hungry Tomato Ltd
F15, Old Bakery Studios, Blewetts Wharf, Malpas Road, Truro, Cornwall, TR1 1QH, UK.

No part of this publication may be reproduced, stored in a retrieval system, or transmitted in any form or by any means, electronic, mechanical, photocopying, recording, or otherwise, without prior written permission of the copyright owner.

A CIP catalogue record for this book is available from the British Library.

ISBN 978 1 915461 74 2

Printed in China

Discover more at
www.hungrytomato.com

Picture Credits:
(abbreviations: t-top; b-bottom; m-middle; l-left; r-right; bg-background)

1, 2-3, 4-5, 6 New Africa; 4, 32 Madezdha f; 6br Petespix; 6bm Anton Starikov; 7m Ortis; 7m kzww; 7bl Quang Ho; 10-11 KN; 12-13 drawkman; 14-17 ladadikart; 18-21 stockvit; 18-21 wisnu bayu aji; 22-25 Natykach Natalia; 26-27 alexdndz; 30-31 vectorsbang.